Misha's Message of PAWSITIVITY

BASED ON A CHOCOLATE LAB'S INSPIRING TRUE STORY OF LOVE, ADVENTURE, LOSS, AND DETERMINATION

By

DANA HOLLIS

Illustrated By

JAMES KOENIG

Misha's Message of Pawsitivity - text and illustrations by Dana Hollis and James Koenig

Dana Hollis
141 Shirley Drive
Charlestown, RI 02813

To Luna and Misha
for always giving me a
reason to wag my tail!

- DANA HOLLIS -

To my pawsitive dog, Bailey,
who's bouncing around
outside right now!

- JAMES KOENIG -

Table of Contents:

Chapter 1

Life with Mom and Dad

"Luna, Luna! Wake up! I just looked outside. It's low tide! You know what that means...Daddy's going clamming!"

It was 5:30 on Saturday morning, but the idea of going clamming woke Luna up in a heartbeat. Luna and I quietly scurried out of the bedroom so we wouldn't wake up Mommy.

We edged each other down the stairs, tumbling onto the floor just as Dad was getting his clamming gear together. He chuckled. Luna and I raced to the front door.

My name is Misha. I'm a chocolate lab. I live with my Mom, Dad, and very best friend and sister, Luna, a black lab.

Dad asked, "Who's ready to go clamming?!"

We both raced to the water. This has always been a favorite adventure of ours. While Dad clammed, we climbed rocks and patrolled the waters for tiny fish and crabs.

Luna and I loved weekends. It meant that we got to spend two whole days with both Mom and Dad. I wondered what we'd do later when Mom was awake.

We went to Rock Island. Rock Island is a cluster of rocks rising out of the water just off shore. There are a lot of things to do there, but my favorite was always jumping off the very top of the rock into the water! The neighborhood kids liked jumping too and laughed when I dove in after them! Luna preferred to watch and bark!

On Sunday afternoon, Mom and Dad took us to the sand bar. At low tide, we ran into the shallow water after birds, sticks, and balls. Dad anchored the boat and let us run on the sand. Then we swam into the deep water. We met a lot of other dogs and their owners there. Everyone had a good time.

Life is good when you live on the coast of Rhode Island!

One day, Mom took us on the kayak. We had just reached Rock Island when a seal popped out of the water. Luna and I instantly dove off the kayak and into the water to play with this new found friend. As soon as I got my head above water, the seal had disappeared. I was worried we had scared her away.

Suddenly, she popped up a few feet away! As Luna and I swam towards her, the seal dove into the water then popped up a few more feet away. She was playing hide and seek with us!

Mom was still sitting in the kayak amazed and giggling as she watched. We would have played all day, but Mom got soaking wet from our splashing. She started to kayak home, knowing we would follow her...and we did, all three of us!

The seal played with us for two weeks. She'd swim to our dock and we'd jump in the water to play.

One sad day, our seal friend didn't stop by our dock to say hello. Dad said that she found other seals to live with. We missed that silly seal, especially Luna.

For days, she would sit on a big rock and scan the surface of the water, hoping for a glimpse of our friend.

Eventually we understood why the seal had to leave.
Before we knew it, Mom and Dad took us on a vacation.

Luna and I wondered where we might be headed. It
turned out to be Florida! We loved Florida because it's a
very dog friendly state. The beaches, the parks, the
restaurants...everyone was always happy to see us!

Our favorite restaurant was called "The Salty Dog."
Whenever we'd arrive, the waitress always presented us
with some cookies and a bowl of water!

When we were there, we felt like V.I.P.'s...
VERY IMPORTANT PUPS!

While we were in Florida, Dad rented a boat. We were speeding along when a dolphin jumped out of the water! We were very excited! It was the greatest thing we had ever seen! Every time we went for a boat ride, dolphins would swim alongside our boat, leap into the air, and dive into the water! It was always so thrilling to watch!

By swimming in the wake or waves of a boat, the dolphins could hitch a ride and move through the water like a surfer. They could be seen weaving back and forth, playing in the spray, and forming patterns in the water.

Their leaps and spins seemed to be a celebration of their joy for life!

❖ CHAPTER 2 ❖

Luna and I Get Sick

When we got home from Florida, Mom took Luna to the Animal Hospital because she had been coughing a lot. The veterinarian took tests and said that she had Cancer. I had no idea what Cancer was, but it sounded scary. I learned that Cancer is an illness that can affect both people and animals.

I was a little less scared when I heard that if it's caught early, it can be treated and sometimes cured. The vet prescribed a special treatment to help fight the Cancer. Mom also made special food to help make Luna healthier. Both the medicine and the food helped.

Although Luna still had Cancer, she felt great due to the treatments. Luna always felt good enough to swim, chase squirrels, and wrestle with me.

For three years, Mom took Luna to the Animal Hospital to make sure she was still doing okay. I always went along for moral support. Most of the time Luna's health was good. If her tests proved otherwise, they would change her medicine and she'd feel better again. During this whole journey, Luna continued to have fun. You would never know she was sick and I was glad to still have my best friend by my side!

One of the most important things that Luna taught me is, whether you are sick, had a bad day, or depressed, there will always be something to wag your tail about!

One ordinary day, Mom noticed that I was limping. Off to the Animal Hospital we went. After the exam, the vet told Mom that I had Cancer in my front leg. This time Luna knew it was her turn to give ME moral support.

He recommended that they amputate my leg so the Cancer wouldn't spread. Mom cried, wishing they wouldn't have to remove my leg, but she knew the procedure would save my life.

Even though I knew I had Cancer, all I thought about was Mom and Dad. For the last three years, they fought this disease with Luna. To find out that I was stricken with Cancer really made them sad.

The day of my surgery came quickly. The vet gave me something to fall asleep. When I woke up, I was in a lot of pain. My front leg was gone. My fur was shaved and I had a bunch of stitches where my leg used to be. It was really hard not to feel depressed.

After a few days, it was time for me to go home. Luna was the first to greet me. I appreciated her support, but I just wanted to be alone.

I usually laid under my favorite tree while recovering. Luna stayed with me until my spirits picked up. Then one day, I realized that Luna wasn't feeling so well.

After three years of fighting Cancer, Luna was losing the battle. It was such a surprise because Luna showed no signs of slowing down until the very end. Losing a leg didn't seem quite so important to me now.

Mom and Dad stayed strong for us. Through their grief, they helped me and also kept Luna as comfortable as possible.

As I got stronger, Luna got weaker. A month after I lost my leg, I lost my sister and my very best friend. We were all heart broken.

REST IN PEACE, LUNA
WE LOVE YOU AND MISS YOU!

CHAPTER 3

Finding Pawsitivity

It wasn't that strange that Luna and I both got Cancer. Animals are very sensitive to toxins, since we are low to the ground. Indoors, we can inhale bad house cleaning chemicals. Outdoors, pesticides in lawn care products can get into our skin and lungs...but who wants to stop rolling in the grass?

Cancer can be prevented if more people use natural, organic cleansers and feed their pets foods that are good for them. If we strive to feed people, animals, and the earth with good things, we can all stay healthy.

I decided that I was not going to let the loss of my leg take away my zest for life. I thought of Luna. She had always enjoyed her life despite her illness. She had the most PAWSITIVE attitude! She was my hero and I chose to begin living by her example.

I was getting stronger every day and before long, my friend Lucky, a golden retriever, arrived for a visit. Although my stitches were out and my hair was growing back, it still shocked him to see me with three legs. Lucky was so upset that he ran to the beach, dug a hole in the sand, and put his head in it! Can you believe that?

It can be upsetting to see a friend who becomes sick or disabled. Friends need to be strong for those going through physical challenges. It just took Lucky a minute to realize that. Although I looked different, I was still the same friend he always loved.

Something amazing happened that day. I watched Lucky and my friends playing on the beach. They were retrieving a stick from the ocean. Before I knew it, I had jumped up and was running down to the water!

I completely forgot that I was missing a leg! Mom threw the stick into the ocean and I was the first to retrieve it! I had the stick and I was swimming...with three legs! That's when I realized that I could still do everything I did before I lost my leg!

I thought of Luna again. She'd be so proud of me! She'd want to see me still enjoying the things I love to do!

I had a new leash on life! My advice...

BE PAWSITIVE!

Live without limits! Let the hard times be an opportunity to show how strong you really are!

NOW I JUST WANTED TO CELEBRATE LIFE...

30

...and perch myself on the bow of a boat,

ride on the paddleboard,

swim,

and leap for the joy of life
like the dolphins do!

I was feeling so confident about my newly earned strength, that one morning I did something unexpected.

Mom and Dad were enjoying a cup of coffee on the front porch, when all of a sudden, a coyote trotted down our driveway from the woods nearby. Luna and I used to hear the coyotes howl in the middle of the night, but I had never seen one bold enough to walk through my neighborhood.

As soon as I saw the coyote, I jumped up and chased it down the driveway, across the street and onto a path that leads into the woods.

Mom ran after me, afraid the coyote was going to turn around, see a three-legged dog chasing it, and decide to fight me. Luckily, I scared that coyote so much that he never came back!

🐾 CHAPTER 4 🐾

Pawsitivity is Contagious

As word spread about my quick and successful recovery, my Mom's friend Kelly approached her. Kelly is a nurse and told Mom that my story would be very inspiring to the kids at the Children's Hospital.

Kelly explained that when children need to heal, a dog can do wonders, especially one that knew all about overcoming challenges!

As a dog myself, I know animals can help in many ways. We can provide a fun distraction as well as emotional support. Dogs sense people's needs and instinctively know how to comfort them. My dog friends and I have always been eager to offer unconditional love and affection.

So Kelly organized time for me to visit the hospital and meet children who were sick, injured, and disabled.

During our visits to the hospital, I noticed one patient's door was always closed. Kelly told Mom that it was Tommy's room. At age fifteen, recruiters had already approached him about playing professional ice hockey. But sadly, due to a recent car accident, Tommy lost his left leg. He was so upset that he refused to see anyone, do therapy, or put on a prosthetic leg.

I knew I had to meet Tommy. I got the chance when a nurse came out of Tommy's room. Quickly, I tugged my leash out of Mom's hand and darted into the room! Tommy looked shocked as I spun around in excitement! I jumped onto the bed, landed on his lap, and started to lick his face. Tommy burst into laughter!

Kelly and Mom came running into the room, followed by Tommy's mother. She hadn't seen Tommy laugh since the accident.

I sat on the bed and enjoyed Tommy's affection. Mom told them my story of loss and recovery. Tommy was surprised to hear that it had happened just a few months ago.

Later Tommy's mom called my Mom. She said that I had inspired him. He didn't feel alone anymore. He thought if a three-legged dog could be so happy and overcome her disability, then so could he. Tommy agreed to try a therapy session with his prosthetic leg and asked if I could be there with him.

I was there every time Tommy had a session. I was also there to comfort him when he got tired and frustrated. As time went on, Tommy got stronger. He said it was my moral support that helped him heal faster!

Through our shared experience of disability, Tommy and I grew very close. Still, Tommy had another hurdle to get over. Emotionally, he was very self-conscious about his prosthetic leg and hesitated to go out if he didn't have to.

Mom made arrangements for us to have lunch with Tommy and his mom at a restaurant on the water. After lunch, she planned a walk along the pier. Although Tommy hesitated, I wiggled around him excitedly until he agreed to walk with me. As we walked, people stopped us. They'd kneel down to pet me and asked what happened to my leg. They were impressed with my Pawsitive attitude! No one even noticed Tommy's prosthetic leg.

Tommy's confidence grew every time we'd go for a walk together. He realized that people weren't treating him any differently than before his accident. He stopped treating himself differently. He realized his worth. A lost leg wasn't going to stop him from enjoying his life.

Now, who does that sound like?

There was one more thing to do...

Mom and Dad invited Tommy and his parents to visit us for a day on the water. It was a beautiful day. We went to Rock Island for a picnic. As usual, some of the neighborhood kids were there jumping off the cliff. They hollered for me to dive off with them. I was excited to show Tommy what I could do!

At this time, Mom and Dad told everyone the story of Luna and myself, the good times and the hard times. They talked about how we all try to live life to the fullest with a Pawsitive attitude despite challenges. Tommy had learned that now. So when I wiggled up to him, he immediately hopped up, and in an instant, like the dolphins in Florida...

we both leaped into the air
to celebrate the joy of life!

This book is based on a true story. Here are some real life pictures of Misha and Luna...

Luna sitting on Rock Island

Misha jumping off the dock

Dad, Misha, and Luna clamming

Luna and Misha's seal friend

ABOUT THE AUTHOR

Dana Hollis is a former Music Industry executive with time spent in New York City and Los Angeles, California. She left her 20-year career after she met and married her husband, Stan. They reside on the coast of Rhode Island. Besides her passion for music, Dana has always had a passion for animals... especially retrievers. She has had Labrador Retrievers all her life. She has volunteered as a foster parent for SAVE A LAB RESCUE, a non-profit organization that is dedicated to the rescue, rehabilitation and rehoming of displaced Labrador Retrievers and Lab mixes. (www.savealabrescue.org) Unfortunately, that came to an end because she kept all the dogs she fostered!

Dana strives to live life the way her dogs have taught her. Greet people with enthusiasm. Make your own fun. Make new friends. Learn new tricks no matter your age. Accept others without judgment. Lick your wounds and shake it off. Unleash your talents. Sniff out opportunities. Chase after your dreams. Love unconditionally.

"A very special thanks to James Koenig for bringing Misha's story to life with his beautiful illustrations! It was an absolute joy working with you!"

-Dana Hollis

About the Illustrator

James Koenig is an illustrator who resides in Arizona. He lives with his wife, Corissa, and dog, Bailey. Bailey is a border collie, golden retriever mix. James and his wife have always loved dogs and so many have been part of the family over the years.

James started drawing almost as soon as he was born. It was always a passion of his and eventually made it a career when he grew up. Whether he has truly grown up is still up for debate. James has illustrated for over 40 books over his career so far. Along with books, he has also developed characters and artwork for countless products, toys, games, and more. You can see more of his work at his website: www.freelancefridge.com.